J
973.7
Ford, Carin

Lincoln's Gettysburg address and the Battle of Gettysburg

LINCOLN's GETTYSBURG ADDRESS AND THE BATTLE OF GETTYSBURG THROUGH PRIMARY SOURCES

Carin T. Ford

Enslow Publishers, Inc.
40 Industrial Road
Box 398
Berkeley Heights, NJ 07922
USA

http://www.enslow.com

Original edition published as *The Battle of Gettysburg and Lincoln's Gettysburg Address* in 2004.

Library of Congress Cataloging-in-Publication Data

Ford, Carin T.
    Lincoln's Gettysburg Address and the Battle of Gettysburg through primary sources / Carin T. Ford.
          p. cm. — (The Civil War through primary sources)
    Rev. ed. of: The Battle of Gettysburg and Lincoln's Gettysburg Address. Berkeley Heights, NJ : Enslow Publishers, © 2004.
    Summary: "Examines the Battle of Gettysburg, including the events leading to the battle, the important people involved, the aftermath and impact on the Civil War, and President Lincoln's Gettysburg Address"—Provided by publisher.
    Includes bibliographical references and index.
    ISBN 978-0-7660-4126-4
    1. Gettysburg, Battle of, Gettysburg, Pa., 1863—Juvenile literature. 2. Lincoln, Abraham, 1809–1865. Gettysburg address—Juvenile literature. I. Ford, Carin T. Battle of Gettysburg and Lincoln's Gettysburg Address. II. Title.
    E475.53.F67 2014
    973.7'349—dc23
                                    2012035626

Future editions:
Paperback ISBN: 978-1-4644-0184-8
EPUB ISBN: 978-1-4645-1097-7
Single-User PDF ISBN: 978-1-4646-1097-4
Multi-User PDF ISBN: 978-0-7660-5726-5

Printed in the United States of America
012013 The HF Group, North Manchester, IN

10 9 8 7 6 5 4 3 2 1

To Our Readers: We have done our best to make sure all Internet Addresses in this book were active and appropriate when we went to press. However, the author and the publisher have no control over and assume no liability for the material available on those Internet sites or on other Web sites they may link to. Any comments or suggestions can be sent by email to comments@enslow.com or to the address on the back cover.

Illustration Credits: Alfred Whital Stern Collection of Lincolniana, Library of Congress Rare Book and Special Collections Division, p. 38; Frank Kovalchek, p. 23; Gettysburg National Military Park, pp. 20, 27; Library of Congress Geography and Map Division, p. 14; Library of Congress Prints and Photographs, pp. 1, 2, 3, 4, 5, 9, 11, 16, 18, 19, 21, 25, 28, 29, 34, 36, 37; Maxime VIGE / Photos.com, p. 41; National Archives and Records Administration, pp. 12, 31; Robert Todd Lincoln Papers, Library of Congress Manuscript Division, p. 33.

Cover Illustration: The Granger Collection, NYC (Illustration of Abraham Lincoln delivering the Gettysburg Address, November 19, 1863).

CONTENTS

---⭐---

LOOK FOR THIS SYMBOL **PRIMARY SOURCE** TO FIND THE PRIMARY SOURCES
THROUGHOUT THIS BOOK.

Joshua Chamberlain, leader of the 20th Maine Infantry, was charged with holding Little Round Top against the Confederate attack. The fighting was bloody, but his troops pushed the Confederates back. This photo shows four dead soldiers in the woods near Little Round Top.

CHAPTER 1

★

INVADING THE NORTH

Joshua Chamberlain did not know what to do. It was July 2, 1863—the second day of fighting in Gettysburg, Pennsylvania. Chamberlain was leader of the 20th Maine Infantry in the Union army. He had been ordered to hold a hill called Little Round Top at all costs. He could not let the Confederates take control of it.

Chamberlain had fewer than 400 soldiers. Most of them were fishermen and lumberjacks. They had no experience in battle. But they were stubborn and willing to fight to the death. Five times the Confederates tried to push them off the hill. Five times they pushed the Confederates back.

"The blood stood in puddles in some places on the rocks," said Confederate colonel William Oates.[1]

The bodies of soldiers who had been killed or wounded lay everywhere. Chamberlain had lost a third of his men after an hour and a half of fighting. The rest of the soldiers had only a few bullets left for their guns. Chamberlain's men could not give up the hill . . . yet how could they stay and fight without bullets?

Suddenly he yelled, "Bayonet!"[2] Each man quickly jammed a steel blade into the muzzle end of his gun. The Maine soldiers then charged wildly down the hill with their bayonets held high—straight at the terrified Southerners.

Chamberlain's plan worked. The Confederates ran away "like a herd of wild cattle," said Oates.[3] The Union had held Little Round Top.

The Battle of Gettysburg lasted three days. It took place halfway through the Civil War. The war had started in April 1861. However, trouble had been brewing between the Northern and Southern states for many years. At the root of the problem was slavery.

Who's Who in the Civil War

★ The North was also known as the Union, or the United States. The people there were often called Yankees.

★ The South was called the Confederate States, or the Confederacy. During the war, Southerners were also called Rebels or Johnny Reb.

For 250 years, slaves had worked on Southern farms and plantations. Slaves planted and harvested the cotton that made money for the South.

Slaves often worked fourteen hours a day in the hot fields. They were not paid. They were treated like property. Many were harshly beaten, and few had enough to eat.

The businesses and small farms of the North did not depend on slaves to do the work. Slavery had been abolished—or ended—in the North years earlier. Many Northerners believed slavery was wrong.

Southerners did not want to get rid of slavery. They worried that President Lincoln, a Northerner, would try to end slavery throughout the United States. Southerners did not think the federal government had the right to tell each state what to do.

Beginning in December 1860, seven Southern states broke away—or seceded—from the rest of the country. They formed their own country, the Confederate States of America. They set up their own government. But President Lincoln was determined to keep the United States together.

Confederate soldiers fired on Union soldiers on April 12, 1861, at Fort Sumter, South Carolina. Soon after, four more states joined the Confederacy. The Civil War began as a battle to bring these states back into the United States, or Union.

Many Northerners thought it would be a short war. They had more men and more guns. Yet during the first two years of fighting, the South won many victories over the Northern soldiers.

Part of the reason was Robert E. Lee. A polite man in his mid-fifties with a neat white beard, Lee was the chief general of

Robert E. Lee

Robert E. Lee graduated with the second highest grades in his class at West Point Military Academy. In early 1861, President Lincoln asked Lee to take command of the Union army. It was a hard decision for Lee. He did not believe in slavery. He also did not think the South should have broken away from the rest of the nation. Still, he would not fight against his home state of Virginia.

"If Virginia stands by the old Union, so will I," he said. "But if she secedes . . . then I will follow my native State with my sword, and if need be with my life."[4]

Lee said no to President Lincoln. Instead, he joined the Confederate army.

General Robert E. Lee

PRIMARY SOURCE

the Confederate armies. He was an excellent military leader, and his men were devoted to him.

By 1863, Lee was eager to invade the North. He came from Virginia, where there had been a lot of fighting.

Lee hoped to draw the fighting away from his war-torn state. Also, Confederate soldiers would be able to find badly-needed food and supplies in the North. Finally, Lee believed that most Northerners were getting tired of the war. He thought that if the South won a major victory in the North, Northerners might want to end the war and make peace with the Confederacy.

In June 1863, Lee led 75,000 men up to central Pennsylvania. General James E. B. "Jeb" Stuart rode ahead of Lee. Stuart led the cavalry—the soldiers on horseback. His job was to scout the area and find out exactly where the Union army was located. Stuart decided to ride around the entire Union army so he could give General Lee a full report.

The Union forces were led by General George G. Meade. Meade had just been made the Union commander a couple of

This bird's-eye view of the battlefield at Gettysburg, drawn in 1863, shows the positions of the Union and Confederate armies during the battle.

General George Meade commanded the Union troops during the Battle of Gettysburg.

days earlier. He had a quick temper and a sharp tongue. Soldiers did not always like Meade, but they respected him.[5]

"I am moving at once against Lee . . . and will settle this thing one way or the other," Meade wrote to his wife.[6]

The Union army was made up of 95,000 men. They were spread out over many miles, and it took Stuart longer than he expected to ride around them. Stuart was not able to get word to Lee about the Union army's position. So General Lee had no idea where the Union army was—or how big it was.

On July 1, Lee's soldiers were just west of Gettysburg, Pennsylvania. It was a hot, sticky day in the hilly farm town, where peaches and wheat grew. Gettysburg was a small town of only 2,400 people. Lee had heard that his soldiers would be able to get shoes there; they needed them badly.[7]

While Lee's men marched, some Union cavalry were scouting the area, looking for Confederate soldiers. In the early hours of the morning, the two groups ran into each other. Fighting broke out on a long hill called McPherson Ridge.

Both sides called quickly for extra help. Soon it arrived: 25,000 Confederate soldiers and 19,000 Union soldiers. The Confederates were able to push the Union troops through the streets of Gettysburg and south of town.

"People were running here and there screaming that the town would be shelled," said Sallie Broadhead, who lived in Gettysburg. "No one knew where to go or what to do."[8]

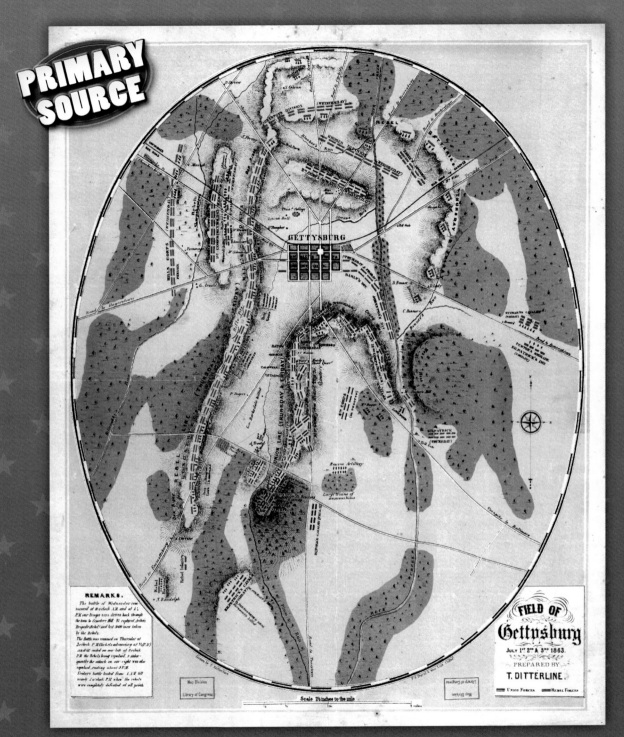

This map of the field at Gettysburg, published in 1863 after the battle, shows troop and artillery positions, roads, railroads, and houses for all three days of the battle.

By nightfall, Lee had lost about 6,500 men. In the Union army, 12,000 soldiers were killed, wounded, or missing.

The Confederates had won the first day of the battle. Yet Meade was pleased with the Union army's position for the following day of fighting. His men were spread out on Culp's Hill and Cemetery Hill. On the high ground, they could easily see the position of the Confederate soldiers. They were ready to fight them off if there was an attack.

The first day of the battle was over. Lee's men were north and west of town. Lee had not yet heard from Stuart. He still did not know where the rest of the Union troops were located, nor how many men there were. But he was determined to continue fighting. "I am going to whip them," he said, "or they are going to whip me."[9]

SECOND DAY OF BATTLE

July 2, 1863, was a cloudy, hot Thursday. Soldiers had arrived throughout the night, making both armies stronger. Lee was eager to attack, although his 65,000 Confederate soldiers would be up against 85,000 Union men. Lee knew he faced a hard task. Yet he did not believe anyone could defeat his army.[1]

Many different battles would take place that day. Lee's main goal was to take the hilly region south of Gettysburg—Little Round Top and Big Round Top.

General James Longstreet led the Confederate attack. He was supposed to start early in the day, but it took him until late afternoon to move his men into position.

Union general Daniel F. Sickles had been ordered by Meade to hold Little Round Top. But Sickles did not like this position. He decided instead to move his troops half a mile forward to high open ground near a peach orchard.[2]

Meade was very angry when he learned what Sickles had done. Now there was no one to defend the Round Tops. Meade ordered Sickles back to Little Round Top, but there was no time. The Confederates had begun their attack.

The fighting was fierce. Meade was as determined as Lee. He quickly sent four regiments to the hill. Longstreet was able to break through the Union line, but his attack was stopped as more Union soldiers arrived at Little Round Top.

The 20th Maine Infantry was the last to arrive. The struggle was bloody. First Lieutenant Charles E. Hazlett was standing near another Union officer, who was suddenly shot in the head. Hazlett leaned forward to catch the dying man's words. Suddenly, he, too, was shot and fell dead on top of the officer. There were many deaths on both sides. But the Union soldiers held on to Little Round Top.

Union general Daniel Sickles was wounded during the second day of fighting when a cannonball struck his leg. Despite the serious injury, Sickles remained calm and helped lead his troops in the fight at the peach orchard, the wheat field, and Devil's Den.

In the peach orchard, Sickles's men were involved in another terrible battle. During the fighting, Sickles was hit by a cannonball. Although his right leg was shattered, the general stayed calm. He smoked a cigar as he was carried from the field.

More soldiers arrived to help Sickles's men fight in the orchard, the wheat field, and Devil's Den.

Second Day of Battle

To the north of these battle sites, the Confederates tried to take Cemetery Ridge and Cemetery Hill. But Union soldiers were able to fight them off.

By the end of the second day of the battle, the Confederates had won some ground at Culp's Hill. Yet the Union lines still held strong. The fighting had been so brutal, it was said that the water in Plum Run stream flowed blood red. People later called this area the Valley of Death. Each army had lost about 9,000 men.

Fierce fighting occurred at many sites on the battlefield at Gettysburg. Artist Alfred R. Waud made this drawing of the fighting at Cemetery Hill during the battle on July 3, 1863.

Primary Source

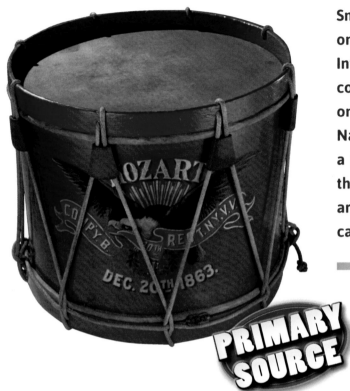

Snare drums, such as this one from the 40th New York Infantry, were used to beat out commands during battle. This one can be seen at Gettysburg National Military Park. After a long second day of fighting, the Union and Confederate armies each had about 9,000 casualties.

Lee and Meade met with their officers that night. They made plans for the next day. So far, the Confederates had attacked the Union army on both its sides . . . and failed.

Meade turned to General John Gibbon, who commanded the troops on Cemetery Ridge, at the center of the Union line. "If Lee attacks tomorrow," Meade said, "it will be in your front."[3]

CHAPTER 3

PICKETT'S CHARGE

Meade was right. Lee planned to have General George Pickett lead the Confederate troops a mile over an open field toward Cemetery Ridge. Richard Ewell would lead a charge to the north of the Union line. Jeb Stuart, who had finally arrived the night before, would lead a cavalry attack from the rear.

The three attacks were supposed to take place at the same time. Yet it was hours before Pickett could get his men into position. Meanwhile, Ewell charged Culp's Hill at four o'clock in the morning. For seven hours, the Confederates fought boldly. At last, they were driven back.

Next came Pickett. He was a dashing Virginian who wore his hair in ringlets. He had graduated from West Point Military Academy with the lowest grades in his class. On that hot and sticky Friday, Pickett believed he would be able to smash through the center of the Union line.

Not everyone thought Lee's plan was a good one. General Longstreet had tried to talk Lee out of it. The 15,000 Confederate soldiers would have little protection as they marched over the wide-open field. In addition, the Union had gotten more men and more ammunition during the night. Their position on the high ground of Cemetery Ridge was strong.

"I have been a soldier all my life," Longstreet told Lee. "It is my opinion that no 15,000 men . . . can take that position."[1]

But Lee would not change his mind. "The enemy is there and I am going to strike him," he said.[2]

Confederate cannons began blasting the Union line around 1 P.M. But all they did was damage some farmland and fill the area with smoke. The Union then set off its own cannons.

Friend Against Friend

Confederate general Lewis A. Armistead and Union general Winfield Scott Hancock had been friends for nearly twenty years. They were forced to lead their men against each other at Gettysburg. Before the Confederate attack on Cemetery Ridge, Armistead said that if he died in battle, he wanted his Bible to be sent to Hancock's wife.

During Pickett's Charge, Armistead was shot. As he lay on the field, he handed a Union soldier his watch and valuables and asked him to give a message to General Hancock. "Tell General Hancock for me that I have done him and done you all an injury which I shall regret the longest day I live."[3]

As it turned out, Hancock, too, was wounded in the battle that day. He recovered, but Armistead died two days later. Today, a monument called "Friend to Friend," shown here, honors these men at Gettysburg National Military Park. It shows Armistead handing his watch to a soldier.

After nearly two hours, the firing stopped.[4] Pickett was eager to begin his charge. He looked at Longstreet, waiting for the command. But Longstreet was too upset to speak. He was certain the attack would fail. He just nodded his head.

"Up men, and to your posts!" Pickett shouted. "Don't forget today that you are from old Virginia."[5]

The 15,000 Confederate soldiers began marching across the field. The Union soldiers were waiting on the hill behind a stone wall. They watched the Confederates approach. Many Union soldiers were filled with wonder and admiration. Pickett's charge was courageous . . . and hopeless.

As soon as the Confederates came closer, the Union guns shot down row after row of soldiers. Often, ten Southerners were killed by a single exploding artillery shell. "We could not help hitting them at every shot," said one Union officer.[6]

A few Confederates briefly made it to the wall. Yet all who did were killed or captured. A Union soldier named Micah said, "What men are these we slaughter like cattle and still they come at us?"[7]

This illustration depicts Pickett's Charge. During this bold Confederate attack, more than 15,000 soldiers marched across the field toward the Union position. Row after row of Southern soldiers were massacred.

Pickett watched as more than half his unit fell, nearly 7,000 soldiers. He finally ordered his men to retreat.

Lee then ordered Pickett to gather his division of men and prepare for an attack by the Union. Pickett said, "General Lee, I *have* no division now."[8] Pickett was miserable about the deaths of his men. "The moans of my wounded boys, the sight of the dead, upturned faces flood my soul with grief," Pickett wrote.[9]

The One Civilian Death

On the morning of July 3, 1863, Jennie Wade of Gettysburg was baking bread.

Her sister had a new baby boy, and Jennie had come to help out. Jennie was kneading dough at her sister's kitchen table when a bullet pierced the door and hit her in the back. She was killed instantly.

Jennie was the only citizen of Gettysburg to be killed in the battle. She was twenty years old.

Lee took full blame for the failed attack. "It's all my fault," he said. He had believed that his men could not be beaten.[10]

The attack became known as Pickett's Charge. It was the end of the Battle of Gettysburg. The Confederate army never again invaded the North.

The cavalry attack, led by Jeb Stuart, failed, too. The soldiers tried to go behind Union lines and attack from the rear. But they were stopped by Union cavalry, led by the young general George Armstrong Custer.

Although the Union army had won the battle, both sides had lost many men. In the Union army, 23,000 soldiers were killed, wounded, missing, or captured. The South had lost almost 28,000 men—one third of Lee's army.

That evening, a Union soldier wrote in his diary, "If ever I was glad to have night come I am tonight."[11]

After Pickett's Charge failed, the three-day battle ended with massive casualties on both sides. This bloodstained diary, on display at Gettysburg National Military Park, belonged to Alfred S. Rowe of Company C, 6th Maryland Volunteer Infantry. It shows a bullet hole through the top.

PRIMARY SOURCE

CHAPTER 4

★

AFTER THE BATTLE

The next day was the Fourth of July. General Lee pulled his soldiers out of Pennsylvania, and they began walking home in the rain to Virginia. His army was in no shape to fight. Still, Lee made sure they were ready in case Union soldiers came after them.

But Meade did not follow Lee into the South. His men were tired, and they had just about run out of food. Meade was content with winning the battle and pushing the Confederates off Northern land.

President Lincoln was furious that Meade did not go after Lee. "Will our generals never get the idea out of their heads?" he asked. "The whole country is our soil."[1]

After the Battle

If Meade had attacked and defeated the Confederates, the Civil War might have ended then. Instead, the fighting dragged on for two more years.

The three-day battle had left the town of Gettysburg in shambles. Crops were destroyed, property was damaged, food was stolen, and houses were robbed. The fields were now covered with thousands of wounded and dead soldiers. The dead bodies were piled one on top of another.

There were thousands of dead, wounded, and missing soldiers after the battle. This photo taken by Alexander Gardner on July 5, 1863, shows the bodies of Confederate soldiers at the edge of Rose Woods in Gettysburg.

PRIMARY SOURCE

"The houses, the barns, the sheds, and the open barnyards were crowded with moaning and wailing human beings . . . " said Union general Carl Schurz. "I saw long rows of men lying under the eaves of the buildings, the [rain] water pouring down their bodies in streams."[2] The fields of Gettysburg were also covered with the bodies of 5,000 dead horses.

It was left to the townsfolk to take the wounded soldiers into their homes, schools, and churches. Tables were quickly set up so doctors could operate on the men. In the fields, blankets were draped over poles to make tents to keep out the rain.

At that time, little was known about medicine or germs. Surgeons often held their knives between their teeth as they prepared to cut off the arms or legs of hundreds of wounded men.

The citizens of Gettysburg, along with hired workers and captured Confederate soldiers, also faced the task of burying the 8,000 dead soldiers. It was a huge job. The bodies were pushed into open ditches, sometimes hundreds at a time. When a soldier's name was known, it was written on a wooden marker and placed near him.

Several days after the battle, Pennsylvania's governor, Andrew G. Curtin, traveled to Gettysburg. The terrible sights and smells shocked him.

Curtin decided to buy land so the men who died in the battle could be properly buried. He put David Wills, a lawyer, in charge. Wills bought some land on the northern slope of Cemetery Hill. It would be divided into different areas for the men of different states.

Wills planned a ceremony to dedicate the cemetery. He invited some famous writers of the day to speak, including poet Henry Wadsworth Longfellow.[3] None were able to attend.

PRIMARY SOURCE

A surgeon at a field hospital in Gettysburg prepares to amputate a limb from a wounded soldier after the battle.

Wills then asked Edward Everett to give a speech. Everett was an important man. In the past, he had been the governor of Massachusetts, a U.S. senator, and the president of Harvard University. About five weeks later, Wills also wrote to President Lincoln, asking if he would come and make "a few . . . remarks."[4]

The ceremony was seventeen days away. This did not give Lincoln much time to write a speech. He made some notes on a piece of paper. There were only eight sentences. When he penciled in a ninth sentence, he needed another piece of paper.

Lincoln made the six-hour trip to Gettysburg on November 18. Traveling with him were several government workers, some army and navy officers, and his friend Ward Lamon.

President and Father

When President Lincoln left home, his wife, Mary, was very upset. Their son Tad was ill. The Lincolns' son Willie had died less than two years earlier, so they were nervous. Fortunately, Tad was feeling better by the time Lincoln returned home.

PRIMARY SOURCE

This is the first page of David Wills' invitation to President Abraham Lincoln, asking if he would make "a few appropriate remarks" at the dedication of the Gettysburg cemetery in November 1863.

Gettysburg Nov. 2nd 1863

To His Excellency
A. Lincoln,
President of the United States,
Sir,
The several States having soldiers in the Army of the Potomac, who were killed at the Battle of Gettysburg, or have since died at the various hospitals, which were established in the vicinity, have procured grounds on a prominent part of the Battle Field for a Cemetery, and are having the dead removed to them and properly buried.

27781

On the train ride, Lincoln talked with the other men for an hour, then said, "Gentlemen, this is all very pleasant, but the people will expect me to say something to them tomorrow, and I must give the matter some thought."[5] He finished making changes to his speech that night at the home of David Wills.

The dedication ceremony took place the next day in front of thousands of people. There was fog and rain. Yet the area was filled with tables at which people were selling cookies, lemonade, and some souvenirs of the battle.

In this illustration, President Lincoln delivers the Gettysburg Address at the dedication of the Gettysburg National Cemetery.

Visitors could buy water canteens, soldiers' buttons, and dead wildflowers from the battlefield.

Wearing a new black suit and black stovepipe hat, Lincoln sat on the wooden platform. He did not feel well; he had a fever.

Everett arrived late. He was the main speaker, and he talked for two hours. He used fancy words to describe the fighting of the past two years. He carefully told the details of each day of the

Gettysburg battle. As Everett was finishing, Lincoln took a piece of paper out of his pocket and silently read it through.

The audience clapped loudly for Everett. Then a chorus sang a hymn for the dead soldiers. As Lincoln stood up, a photographer began to set up his camera.

Lincoln started his speech, making some changes as he spoke.[6] A little more than two minutes later, he was done. Many historians say that the audience was so surprised, they barely clapped. The photographer had not even had time to get the cap off his camera lens.[7] Other historians say his speech was interrupted many times by applause.[8]

In fact, there is no picture of Lincoln delivering the Gettysburg Address. None of the newspaper reporters had time to take many notes.

The president unhappily sat down. "It is a flat failure and the people are disappointed," he said to his friend Lamon.[9]

CHAPTER 5

REMEMBRANCE

On the evening of November 19, 1863, Lincoln took the train back to Washington, D.C. He was tired and ill. Lincoln lay down on his seat with a wet towel across his eyes.

The following day, Everett's speech made the front pages of the newspapers. Lincoln's speech was printed on the inside pages. Although many newspapers praised the speech, the *London Times* said Lincoln was "dull and commonplace."[1] The *Chicago Times* called his speech "silly."[2]

Today, it has become one of the most famous speeches in the nation's history.

Although the Gettysburg Address is now one of the most famous speeches in American history, at the time Lincoln gave it he received some criticism. This photo of Lincoln was taken on November 8, 1863, just eleven days before the speech.

PRIMARY SOURCE

PRIMARY SOURCE

Four score and seven years ago our fathers brought forth on this continent, a new nation, conceived in Liberty, and dedicated to the proposition that all men are created equal.

Now we are engaged in a great civil war, testing whether that nation, or any nation so conceived and so dedicated, can long endure. We are met on a great battle field of that war. We have come to dedicate a portion of that field, as a final resting place for those who here gave their lives that that nation might live. It is altogether fitting and proper that we should do this.

But, in a larger sense, we can not dedicate— we can not consecrate— we can not hallow— this ground. The brave men, living and dead, who struggled here, have consecrated it, far above our poor power to add or detract. The world will little note, nor long remember what we say here, but it can never forget what they did here. It is for us the living, rather, to be dedicated here to the unfinished work which they who fought here have thus far so nobly advanced. It is rather for us to be here dedicated to the great task remaining before us— that from these honored dead we take increased devotion to that cause for which they gave the last full measure of devotion— that we here highly resolve that these dead shall not have died in vain— that this nation, under God, shall have a new birth of freedom— and that government of the people, by the people, for the people, shall not perish from the earth.

Executive Mansion, Washington

November 19. 1863.

Abraham Lincoln.

This is a copy of the Gettysburg Address in Lincoln's handwriting on an envelope.

Lincoln's speech contained about 270 words. He said the nation should live up to the idea that "all men are created equal." The Civil War was a test. Could a government based on treating all people equally survive?[3]

Lincoln did not mention any person by name in his speech. He did not talk about slavery, the Union, or the Confederacy. He did not even mention Gettysburg.[4] Lincoln spoke about honoring the men who had died. He said they gave their lives to keep the

The Gettysburg Address

Four score and seven years ago, our fathers brought forth on this continent, a new nation, conceived in liberty, and dedicated to the proposition that all men are created equal.

Now we are engaged in a great civil war, testing whether that nation, or any nation so conceived and so dedicated, can long endure. We are met on a great battle-field of that war. We have come to dedicate a portion of that field, as a final resting place for those who here gave their lives that the nation might live. It is altogether fitting and proper that we should do this.

But, in a larger sense, we cannot dedicate—we cannot consecrate—we cannot hallow—this ground. The brave men, living and dead, who struggled here, have consecrated it, far above our poor power to add or detract. The world will little note, nor long remember what we say here, but it can never forget what they did here. It is for us the living, rather, to be dedicated here to the unfinished work which they who fought here have thus far so nobly advanced. It is rather for us to be here dedicated to the great task remaining before us—that from these honored dead we take increased devotion to that cause for which they gave the last full measure of devotion—that we here highly resolve that these dead shall not have died in vain—that this nation, under God, shall have a new birth of freedom, and that government of the people, by the people, for the people, shall not perish from the earth.

United States together as one nation. Gettysburg stood for a new birth of freedom throughout the nation.

Everett liked the president's speech. He told Lincoln that he wished he had spoken as well "in two hours as you did in two minutes."[5]

When Lincoln gave the Gettysburg Address, only a part of the cemetery had been finished. It was hard finding out the names of all the men who had died. More than 1,600 soldiers could not be named. They were buried as unknown soldiers. The cemetery was finally finished on March 18, 1864.

The loss at Gettysburg was a heavy blow to the Confederacy. It became even weaker when Confederate soldiers surrendered to Union soldiers at Vicksburg, Mississippi, on July 4. Port Hudson, Louisiana, fell several days later. Then the Union controlled the Mississippi River. The Confederacy had been split in half.

The Civil War came to an end in the spring of 1865. On April 9, General Lee surrendered to Union general Ulysses S. Grant in Appomattox, Virginia. Soon after, the rest of the Confederate armies laid down their weapons.

The Battle of Gettysburg is the most famous battle in American history.[6] More than a million people visit Gettysburg each year. There they can see the statues and monuments that honor the men from the North and the South who gave their lives for their beliefs.

An aerial view of the Gettysburg National Cemetery. The Gettysburg National Military Park gets more than a million visitors each year.

TIMELINE

1860

November 6: Abraham Lincoln is elected president.

December 20: South Carolina secedes from the United States.

1861

February: Six more Southern states secede; the Confederacy is formed.

April 12: Shots are fired at Fort Sumter; Civil War begins.

April–June: Four more Southern states secede.

July 21: The Union is defeated at the First Battle of Bull Run.

1862

March 8–9: Battle between two ironclad ships, *Monitor* and *Merrimack*.

June 1: Robert E. Lee becomes commander of the Confederate army.

August 28–30: The Union is defeated at the Second Battle of Bull Run.

September 17: Union victory at Antietam.

1863

January 1: Lincoln issues Emancipation Proclamation.

May 15: Lee plans invasion of the North.

June 3: Lee's army marches northward.

June 28: Meade takes over Army of the Potomac.

July 1: Battle of Gettysburg begins with fighting on the outskirts of town.

July 2: Union lines remain strong; 20th Maine holds Little Round Top.

July 3: Pickett's Charge fails; Battle of Gettysburg ends in Union victory.

July 4: Lee's army heads back to Virginia.

July 4 and 9: Grant captures Vicksburg and then Port Hudson for the Union. The Confederacy is split in two.

November 19: President Lincoln gives the Gettysburg Address.

1864

March: Ulysses S. Grant is named commander of the Union army.

July: William T. Sherman captures Atlanta for the Union.

November–December: Sherman begins his "March to the Sea."

November 8: Lincoln is reelected for another term as president.

1865

April: Petersburg and Richmond fall to the Union.

April 9: Confederate general Robert E. Lee surrenders to Union general Ulysses S. Grant.

April 14: President Lincoln is assassinated.

April 15: Andrew Johnson becomes president.

CHAPTER NOTES

CHAPTER 1. INVADING THE NORTH

1. Shelby Foote, *The Civil War: A Narrative. Fredericksburg to Meridian* (New York: Random House, 1963), p. 504.
2. Noah Andre Trudeau, *Gettysburg: A Testing of Courage* (New York: HarperCollins Publishers, 2002), p. 370.
3. Geoffrey C. Ward, *The Civil War: An Illustrated History* (New York: Knopf, 1990), p. 221.
4. Winston S. Churchill, *The Great Republic: A History of America* (New York: Modern Library, 2000), p. 151.
5. A. Wilson Greene and Gary W. Gallagher, *National Geographic Guide to the Civil War: National Battlefield Parks* (Washington, D.C.: National Geographic Society, 1992), p. 81.
6. Howard K. Pfanz, *Gettysburg: The First Day* (Chapel Hill, N.C.: The University of North Carolina Press, 2001), p. 43.
7. Ibid., p. 51.
8. Ward, p. 216.
9. Foote, p. 480.

CHAPTER 2. SECOND DAY OF BATTLE

1. William K. Kingaman, *Abraham Lincoln and the Road to Emancipation* (New York: Viking, 2001), p. 258.
2. Gary W. Gallagher, ed., *Three Days at Gettysburg* (Kent, Ohio: Kent State University Press, 1999), p. 140.
3. Shelby Foote, *The Civil War: A Narrative. Fredericksburg to Meridian* (New York: Random House, 1963), p. 525.

CHAPTER 3. PICKETT'S CHARGE

1. Edward J. Stackpole, *They Met at Gettysburg* (Harrisburg, Pa.: Stackpole Books, 1956), p. 245.
2. Charles Carleton Coffin, *Eyewitness to Gettysburg* (Thorndike, Maine: G.K. Hall & Co., 1997), p. 149.
3. <http://home.epix.net/~rplr/gettys3.htm> (June 27, 2003).
4. Shelby Foote, *The Civil War: A Narrative. Fredericksburg to Meridian* (New York: Random House, 1963), p. 549.
5. Geoffrey C. Ward, *The Civil War: An Illustrated History* (New York: Knopf, 1990), p. 228.
6. Ibid., p. 232.
7. Jeffrey D. Wert, *Gettysburg: Day Three* (New York: Simon & Schuster, 2001), p. 302.

8. Ward, p. 236.

9. Arthur Crew Inman, ed., *Soldier of the South: General Pickett's War Letters to His Wife* (Temecula, Calif.: Reprint Services Corp., 1928).

10. Foote, p. 569.

11. Wert, p. 287.

CHAPTER 4. AFTER THE BATTLE

1. Bruce Catton, *Gettysburg: The Final Fury* (New York: Doubleday, 1974), p. 101.

2. "The Ghastly Work of Field Surgeons," *Civil War Home*, n.d., <http://www.civilwarhome.com/fieldsurgeons.htm> (June 27, 2003).

3. Garry Wills, *Lincoln at Gettysburg: The Words that Remade America* (New York: Simon & Schuster, 1992), p. 23.

4. "Gettysburg Address," *Library of Congress*, n.d., <http://www.loc.gov/exhibits/gadd/gainv1.html> (June 27, 2003).

5. Shelby Foote, *The Civil War: A Narrative. Fredericksburg to Meridian* (New York: Random House, 1963), p. 830.

6. William K. Kingaman, *Abraham Lincoln and the Road to Emancipation* (New York: Viking, 2001) p. 271.

7. Foote, 832.

8. Wills, p. 36.

9. Foote, p. 832.

CHAPTER 5. REMEMBRANCE

1. Geoffrey C. Ward, *The Civil War: An Illustrated History* (New York: Knopf, 1990), p. 262.

2. Shelby Foote, *The Civil War: A Narrative. Fredericksburg to Meridian* (New York: Random House, 1963), p. 832.

3. Kent Gramm, *November: Lincoln's Elegy at Gettysburg* (Bloomington, Ind.: Indiana University Press, 2001), pp. 136–137.

4. Garry Wills, *Lincoln at Gettysburg: The Words that Remade America* (New York: Simon & Schuster, 1992), p. 37.

5. <http://www.americaslibrary.gov/cgi-big/page.cgi/jb/civil/gettysbg-3.htm> (June 27, 2003).

6. A. Wilson Greene and Gary W. Gallagher, *National Geographic Guide to the Civil War: National Battlefield Parks* (Washington, D.C.: National Geographic Society, 1992), p. 80.

GLOSSARY

address—A speech.

ammunition—Bullets or other explosives shot from guns or cannons.

artillery—Large firing weapons, such as cannons.

cavalry—Soldiers trained to fight on horseback.

Confederate States of America—The new nation formed by eleven Southern states in 1861 (also called the Confederacy). These states were South Carolina, Alabama, Florida, Mississippi, Louisiana, Texas, Georgia, Virginia, Arkansas, Tennessee, and North Carolina.

dedicate—To show to the public for the first time. To set apart for a special use.

federal—The central government of a union of states.

infantry—Soldiers trained to fight on foot.

line—Military troops arranged side by side.

retreat—Withdrawal of military troops from a dangerous situation.

secede—To withdraw or break away from.

shell—A hollow tube that holds explosives.

troop—A group of soldiers.

West Point Military Academy—A military school started in 1802 to train men to be army officers. (Starting in 1976, women could attend, too.)

FURTHER READING

Books

Fradin, Dennis Brindell. *The Battle of Gettysburg.* New York: Marshall Cavendish Benchmark, 2008.

Gregory, Josh. *Gettysburg.* New York: Children's Press, 2012.

Johnson, Jennifer. *Pickett's Charge at Gettysburg: A Bloody Clash in the Civil War.* New York: Scholastic, Inc., 2011.

Weber, Jennifer L. *Summer's Bloodiest Days: The Battle of Gettysburg as Told From All Sides.* Washington, D.C.: National Geographic, 2010.

Internet Addresses

Civil War.org: Battle of Gettysburg
<http://www.civilwar.org/battlefields/gettysburg.html>

Gettysburg National Military Park
<http://www.nps.gov/gett/index.htm>

INDEX